Annual Report on Vital Signs Monitoring Of Moose (*Alces alces*) Distribution and Abundance in Yukon-Charley Rivers National Preserve, Central Alaska Network, November 2009 Survey Report

Natural Resource Technical Report NPS/CAKN/NRTR—2010/331

John Burch
National Park Service
Yukon-Charley Rivers National Preserve
4175 Geist Road
Fairbanks, AK 99709
John_Burch@NPS.GOV

May 2010

U.S. Department of the Interior
National Park Service
Natural Resource Program Center
Fort Collins, Colorado

The National Park Service, Natural Resource Program Center publishes a range of reports that address natural resource topics of interest and applicability to a broad audience in the National Park Service and others in natural resource management, including scientists, conservation and environmental constituencies, and the public.

The Natural Resource Report Series is used to disseminate high-priority, current natural resource management information with managerial application. The series targets a general, diverse audience, and may contain NPS policy considerations or address sensitive issues of management applicability.

All manuscripts in the series receive the appropriate level of peer review to ensure that the information is scientifically credible, technically accurate, appropriately written for the intended audience, and designed and published in a professional manner.

This report received informal peer review by subject-matter experts who were not directly involved in the collection, analysis, or reporting of the data. Data in this report were collected and analyzed using methods based on established, peer-reviewed protocols and were analyzed and interpreted within the guidelines of the protocols.

Views, statements, findings, conclusions, recommendations, and data in this report are those of the author(s) and do not necessarily reflect views and policies of the National Park Service, U.S. Department of the Interior. Mention of trade names or commercial products does not constitute endorsement or recommendation for use by the National Park Service.

This report is available from The National Park Service, Central Alaska Network website (http://science.nature.nps.gov/im/units/cakn) and the Natural Resource Publications Management website (http://www.nature.nps.gov/publications/NRPM).

NPS 191/102388, May 2010.

Contents

Figures

Executive Summary

- Survey dates: November 17-21, 2009 (4.5 days of survey, 0.5 weather days)

- Total survey area: 3,096 mi^2 (8,019 km^2), 555 survey units

- Area surveyed: 618 mi^2 (1601 km^2), 111 survey units

- Total moose observed: 308 (164 cows, 42 calves [4 set of twins], 102 bulls [21 spike-fork bulls])

- Applied sightability correction factor = 1.2 (ADF&G radiotelemetry studies, GMU 20A, 2007)

- Average search effort: 6.72 minutes/mi^2 (2.59 minutes/km^2)

- *Population estimate: 1331 moose +/- 251 (1080 – 1582) (+/-18.88% at 90% CI)
          (717 cows, 189 calves, 425 bulls [86 spike-fork (yrl) bulls])

- *Estimated density: 0.429 moose/mi^2 (0.166 moose/km^2)

- *Estimated age/sex ratios: 26 calves:100 cows, 27 yearlings:100 cows, 59 bulls:100 cows

- Average harvest: 26 bulls per year (20 year average, preserve wide)

* 1.2 sightability correction factor applied

Key Words
Yukon-Charley Rivers National Preserve, moose, *Alces alces*, Aerial moose survey, population dynamics, GeoSpatial population estimation

Acknowledgments

This survey was funded by U.S. National Park Service, Central Alaska Network Vital Signs Monitoring Program, and Yukon-Charley Rivers National Preserve, Alaska. Many safe flight hours and aircraft support were provided during the survey by pilots Sandy Hamilton, Colin Milone, Dennis Miller, and Seth McMillan, and their help was greatly appreciated. Jori Welchans, Tom Meier, Heidi Kristenson and John Burch served as observers in aircraft. Pat Sanders and Lou Flynn provided communications support in Eagle. Tom Meier made a number of valuable suggestions on earlier drafts of this report.

Introduction

The Central Alaska Network of National Park Service conducted an aerial moose survey during November 17-21, 2009, in Yukon-Charley Rivers National Preserve (YUCH), Alaska (Figure 1).

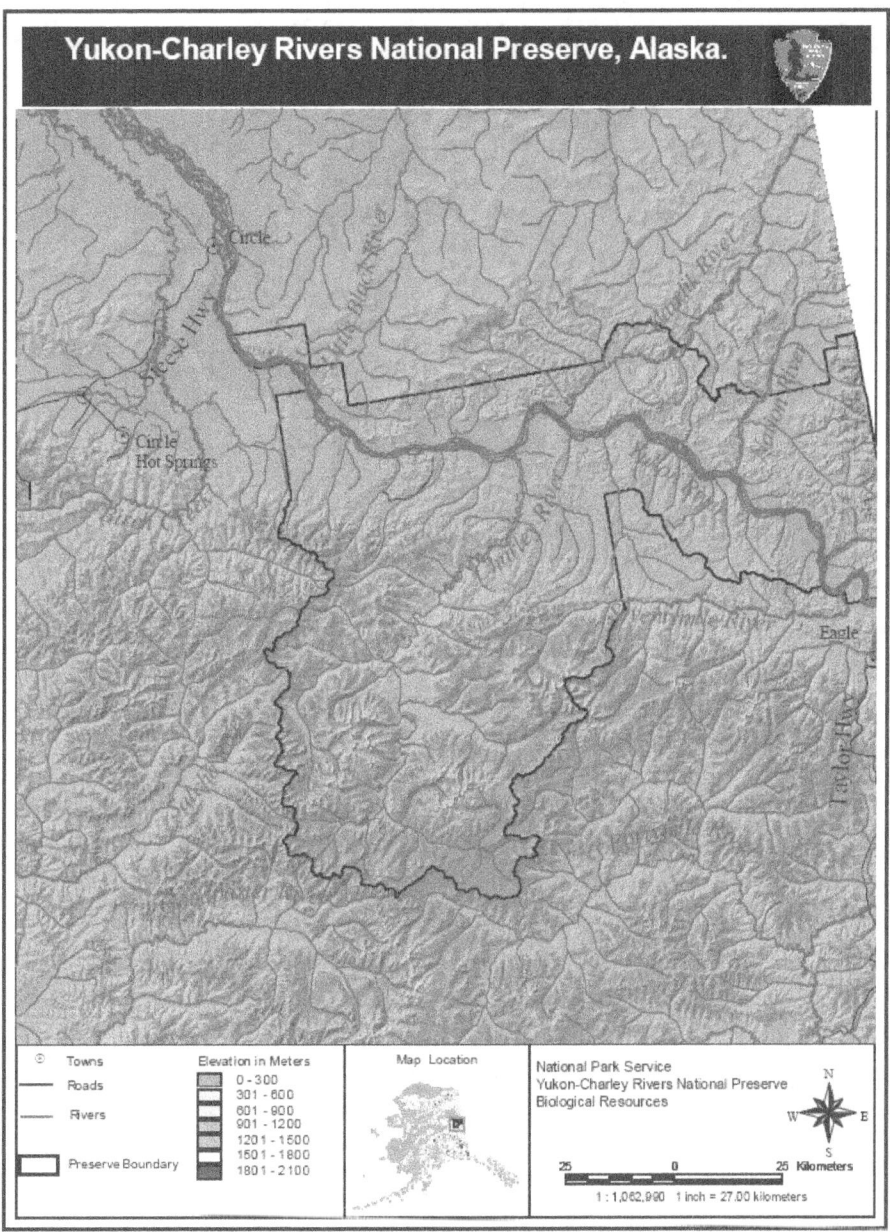

Figure 1. Location of Yukon-Charley Rivers National Preserve (YUCH), Alaska.

The purpose of this survey was to estimate the moose population size and sex/age composition for the Yukon River corridor within YUCH. Moose population information is needed by

Preserve and state wildlife managers for monitoring long-term population trends and to make informed decisions regarding proposed changes to moose hunting regulations for this area. Several moose surveys have been conducted within the preserve during the last 34 years. In February 1975, a brief aerial survey was conducted along the Yukon River to identify winter habitat (Boertje 1985). During 1982-1987, trend counts were conducted in the Washington Creek area as part of an Alaska Department of Fish and Game (ADF&G) study investigating the role of predation in limiting moose densities in east-central Alaska (Gasaway et al. 1992). In November 1987, a large area along the Yukon River was surveyed between Eagle and Circle within YUCH (Nowlin 1988). A winter, moose habitat-use survey was conducted along the lower Nation River and Hard Luck Creek in March 1991 (Knuckles 1991). The entire Charley River drainage and the Yukon River corridor between Glenn Creek and Woodchopper Creek was surveyed in November 1994 (Demma et al. 1995). Sampling methodologies used during these past surveys varied. Consequently, the results of the older surveys (1970s, early 1980s, and 1994) are of limited use in determining long-term moose population changes in YUCH. The same Yukon River corridor area between Eagle and Circle, surveyed in 1987, was surveyed in 1997 (Burch and Demma 1997), 1999 (Burch 1999), 2003 (Burch 2003), 2006 (Burch 2006) and again during this survey, thus providing 6 surveys covering the same area that are directly comparable. This survey and the 2003 and 2006 surveys used the geo-spatial estimator (Ver Hoef 2001, Ver Hoef 2002, Kellie and DeLong 2006). The previous 3 surveys (1987, 1997, 1999) used methods described by Gasaway et al. (1986) and surveyed the same area. All 6 surveys are directly comparable. In 1998, proposals to change harvest regulations were submitted by local subsistence hunters in Eagle. These proposed changes included a longer fall season and the addition of a March hunting season for qualified federal subsistence users. The longer fall season was adopted, but the March season was not. In the past, residents of local communities have relied on caribou from the Fortymile Caribou Herd and moose. The total harvest limit for Fortymile Caribou Herd caribou was reduced from 450 to 150 between 1996 and 2000 as a result of an interagency management plan developed to restore the caribou herd to its former range (ADF&G 1995). The reduction in harvest limits for caribou in the Fortymile Caribou Herd reduced the availability of caribou from this herd for all Alaska residents. Because of this harvest reduction, local residents were more dependent on moose. Harvest opportunity of Fortymile caribou has now increased incrementally beginning in 2001 as outlined in the Fortymile caribou harvest plan (ADF&G, et al 2000, 2006) and has likely taken some human harvest pressure off YUCH's moose population. In spring 2006 the Board of Game endorsed a new Fortymile harvest management plan providing additional caribou harvest opportunity, further reducing harvest pressure on the moose population. Despite this probable reduction in pressure, local residents have voiced concerns of competing with increasing numbers of non-local hunters for area moose during the general hunting seasons. The issue of subsistence vs. general hunting, and issues related to rural preference for local wildlife resources are controversial statewide. Resource conflicts of this nature will likely intensify as competition increases for limited wildlife resources in Alaska. Information provided by this survey (and others like it in the future) will assist managers in effectively evaluating future proposals regarding moose hunting and the moose population inhabiting YUCH. Regularly recurring fall surveys are crucial to monitoring this moose population. Analyses presented here indicate an increase in moose harvested and an increase in the number of people hunting in the Preserve. This increased harvest pressure is on a low density moose population, with poor recruitment most years. This most recent survey indicates a modest increase in population size. However, past surveys indicate a low density, stable population, but the stability of the population is uncertain. Another survey in fall 2012 is planned.

Incorporation of Moose Surveys into the Central Alaska Network (CAKN)

The Central Alaska Network (CAKN) has identified Fauna Distribution and Abundance as one of its top three vital signs. In general, CAKN wants to know where fauna are distributed across the landscape and to track changes in both their distribution and abundance. The Fauna Distribution and Abundance vital sign includes monitoring efforts for a suite of vertebrate species spanning the significant elevation gradient found in CAKN parks, and also including species of specific interest within each park. Moose (*Alces alces*), occur in all three network parks and are one of six large mammal species in interior Alaska. Moose are of great importance to people from both consumptive and non-consumptive viewpoints, and to the ecosystem as a whole. From a monitoring standpoint, moose are considered to be good indicators of long-term habitat change within park ecosystems because they depend on large scale, healthy habitats for food and cover, which in turn are dependent on weather and other habitat patterns across the entire landscape. As a top herbivore, moose may play a key role in influencing vegetation growth and change potentially resulting in habitat change on a landscape scale. Changes in moose populations directly affect subsistence harvest on NPS Park and Preserve lands in Alaska, and harvest by the general public on NPS Preserve lands (National Park Service 2003).

Moose are a species specifically identified in the enabling legislation and management objectives of all three CAKN parks (U. S. Congress 1980). Moose are important to park visitors because of the opportunities to view and hunt moose in Alaskan Parks and Preserves. While the primary objectives of monitoring are to track the distribution and abundance of moose in YUCH, these data are likely to be valuable for wildlife management and research throughout most of interior Alaska. Data on moose populations in Alaska parks is critical for managing those populations for both visitor enjoyment and human harvest.

Study Area

The moose survey was conducted along a 30-40 mile (48-64 km) wide corridor of the Yukon River drainage within YUCH, between Eagle and Circle, Alaska (Figure 2). The topography of the area consists mainly of rolling hills and river bluffs (Figure 3). Isolated rugged terrain occurs on several eroded mountains, with peaks generally under 6000 feet (1200 meters). Vegetation is dominated by black spruce (*Picea mariana*), and several species of deciduous hardwoods including aspen (*Populus tremuloides*) and birch (*Betula papyrifera*). Ponds, sloughs and large areas of tussock tundra are common in the flats along the Yukon River and lower parts of large tributaries such as the Charley and Kandik Rivers. Wildfire burns of varying sizes and ages are present throughout the study area (NPS 1985) (Figure 9) including the more recent large fires from summer 1999 and 2004 along the Yukon, Nation and Kandik rivers. The Preserve's fire management plan (NPS 1999) contains a more in depth review of fire history for the area. YUCH's General Management Plan (National Park Service 1985) and an ecological unit mapping report (Swanson 1999) provide more thorough descriptions of the vegetation and physiography of the area.

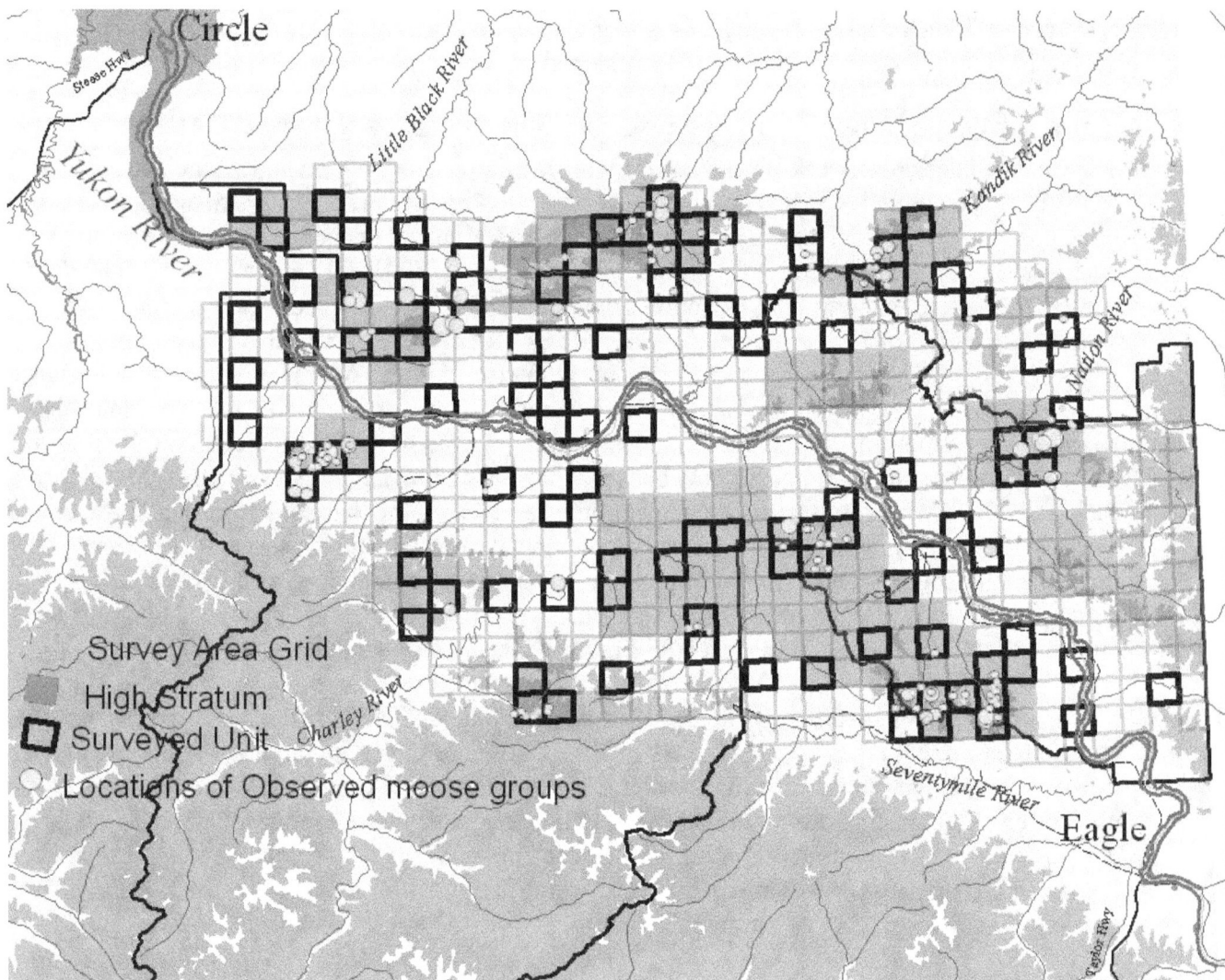

Figure 2. Location of the moose survey area and all survey units (light blue grid). Locations of moose groups observed during the 2009 survey are depicted as green dots. The smallest dots are single moose, largest dots are groups of 6 – 9 moose (the largest seen). Clear units were low stratum and red units were high stratum. Units (111 of them) with heavy black outline were surveyed in November 2009. Yukon-Charley Rivers National Preserve, Alaska.

Figure 3. Typical topography and vegetation of the survey area. Mouth of the Kandik River on Yukon River.

Methods

This survey, a geo-spatial estimator, used methods described by Ver Hoef (2001), Ver Hoef (2002), Kellie and DeLong (2006) and Gasaway et al. (1986). Beginning In 2003, to follow the modifications suggested by Ver Hoef, the study area was reconfigured into a grid of 555 roughly square survey units, from the larger Gasaway style units based on drainages and topography (Figure 4). Each new survey unit averaged 5.58 mi^2. Units were delineated by 2 minutes of latitude by 5 minutes of longitude (Figure 4). Sample units were stratified into high (3 or more moose) or low (0 - 2 moose) moose densities based on moose locations from previous surveys, locations of wolf-killed moose, and knowledge of the local area. Stratification flights (Nowlin 1988, Demma et al. 1995, Burch and Demma 1997, Burch 1999) were not flown during 2003, 2006, or 2009. During the survey, up to four pilot/observer teams, in Piper PA-18, or Christen Husky aircraft surveyed sample units at a rate averaging 6.7 minutes per mi^2 (2.6 minutes/km^2). Moose observed were assigned group numbers and mapped by recording coordinates of each group utilizing the aircraft's Global Positioning System (GPS) receivers. Numbers of moose in each group were recorded and the sex and age classification of each moose was determined. Moose were classified as: cow, calf, yearling bull (spike or forked antlers), medium bull (antler spread > spike/fork, but < 50 inches [127 cm]), and large bull (antler spread ≥50 inches [127 cm]). Total moose, moose density and sex/age ratios were calculated using the GeoSpatial Population Estimator software (DeLong 2006, Kellie and Delong 2006). The software 'MOOSEPOP' (Gasaway et al. 1986, Reed 1989), was used each night at our field camp (Coal Creek Camp) to track the survey's progress and variability as the GeoSpatial software is not yet available 'off line'.

Sightability Correction Factor (SCF)

The GeoSpatial method assumes 100% sightability of moose during a survey (Ver Hoef 2001; Ver Hoef pers. comm., Kellie and DeLong 2006). The reality is something less. Previous stratified random surveys (Gasaway style) missed between 10% and 20% of the moose as measured by 30 – 40 intensive (12^+ minutes/mi^2) survey plots for each moose survey (40% of total plots surveyed). Tests run by Gasaway et al. (1986) indicate that on average, for early winter surveys, 98% of the moose are seen when surveying at a rate of 12 minutes/mi^2, and approximately 90% – 95% are seen when flying at a rate of 7 minutes/mi^2 in interior Alaska. This survey averaged 6.7 minutes/mi^2 of search time. ADF&G has been conducting tests in GMU 20A with radiocollared moose, finding that more than 20% of the moose are missed in forested areas, and some moose are not seen at all even at the highest survey intensities.

ADF&G is now applying a sightability correction factor (SCF) of about 1.2 to the GeoSpatial estimates for GMU 20A (unpublished data, Don Young, pers. comm. 2007, 5/22/2007 ADF&G Memo). A SCF of 1.2 has been applied to the results of this survey and the past Geo-spatial surveys in 2003 and 2006.

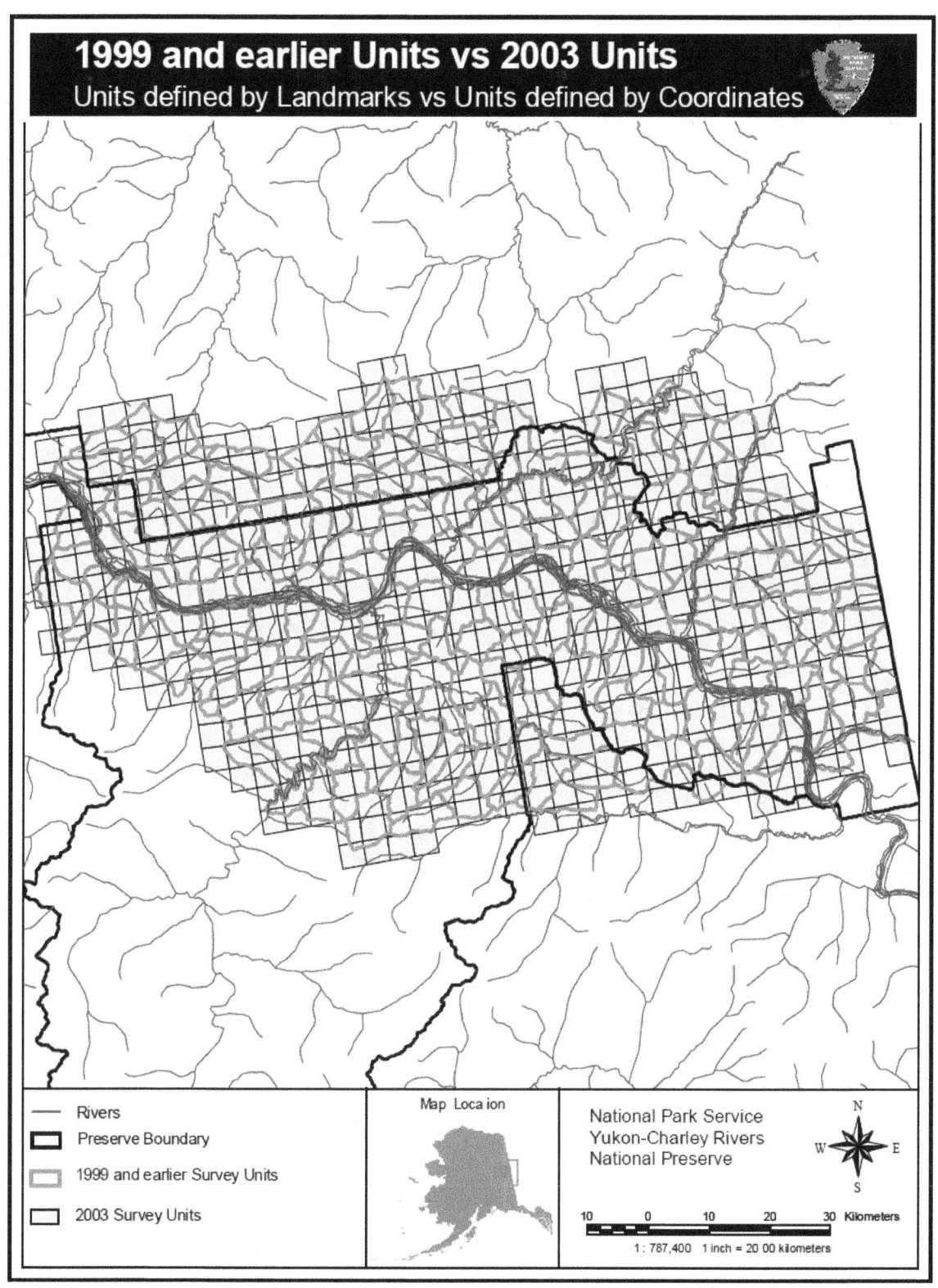

1999 and earlier Units vs 2003 Units
Units defined by Landmarks vs Units defined by Coordinates

Rivers
Preserve Boundary
1999 and earlier Survey Units
2003 Survey Units

Map Loca ion

National Park Service
Yukon-Charley Rivers
National Preserve

N
W E
S

10   0   10   20   30 Kilometers

1 : 787,400   1 inch = 20 00 kilometers

Figure 4 Survey units from 1987, 1997 and 1999 surveys (based on Gasaway et al 1986) compared to the units for the 2003, 2006 and 2009 surveys (as modified by Ver Hoef 2001) in Yukon-Charley Rivers National Preserve, Alaska.

Results and Discussion

Weather and Snow conditions

The weather conditions for flying the survey were good to excellent. Survey flights were stopped for a half day due to local area fog in the river corridor. There were also occasions on the last 2 days of survey when wind prevented surveying in isolated areas in the east end but this did not significantly affect the survey. Snow conditions and sightability were good to excellent throughout the survey area even though only 6 inches (15 cm) of fresh snow covered the study area at the start of the survey. The snow conditions and frost in the trees and bushes remained excellent throughout the survey, producing very good sightability.

General Survey Results

One hundred and eleven of 555 survey units were surveyed, covering 20% of the survey area (Table 1, Figure 2). A total of 69 hours (4,158 minutes) of flight time was spent searching for moose for an average of 37.46 minutes per survey unit. Search intensity averaged 6.72 minutes per mi^2 (2.59 minutes/km^2). A total of 308 moose were observed (164 cows, 42 calves [including 4 sets of twins], and 102 bulls [including 21 spike/fork (yearling bulls)]) (Table 1).

Population Estimate

Extrapolating observed moose numbers and composition to the entire survey area via the GeoSpatial statistics in SMOOSE and applying a Sightability Correction Factor (SCF) of 1.2 (20%) (calculated from previous surveys and ADF&G tests with radiocollared moose) generates an overall estimated density of 0.429 moose/mi^2 (0.166 moose/km^2) and a point estimate of 1331 moose in the 3,096 mi^2 (8,019 km^2) study area (+/- 251 moose (1080 – 1582 or +/-18.88% @ 90% CI); (Table 2, Appendix A). The composition of the estimated 1331 moose was: 717 cows, 189 calves, 425 bulls (of which 86 were spike/fork/yearling bulls).

Table 1. November 2009 moose survey results from surveyed units, Yukon-Charley Rivers National Preserve, Alaska.

Unit	SE Corner Coordinates	Stratum	Area Mi²	Bulls			Cows			Lone Calf	Unk	Total Moose	Search Time	Effort Min/Mi²
				Yrl	Med	Lrg	0calf	1calf	2calf					
32	6534-14240	H	5.519	0	0	0	0	1	0	0	0	2	27	4.89
230	6520-14320	L	5.568	0	0	0	0	0	0	0	0	0	27	4.85
24	6534-14325	L	5.519	0	0	0	0	0	0	0	0	0	28	5.07
39	6534-14205	L	5.519	0	1	0	0	0	0	0	0	1	28	5.07
63	6532-14205	L	5.526	0	0	0	1	1	0	0	0	3	28	5.07
203	6522-14255	L	5.561	0	0	0	0	0	0	0	0	0	28	5.04
107	6528-14305	L	5.54	0	0	0	4	0	0	0	0	4	29	5.23
75	6530-14315	L	5.533	1	1	0	3	0	0	0	0	5	31	5.60
26	6534-14315	L	5.519	0	0	0	0	0	0	0	0	0	31	5.62
7	6536-14345	L	5.512	0	0	0	0	0	0	0	0	0	33	5.99
51	6532-14305	L	5.526	1	3	0	0	0	0	0	0	4	33	5.97
204	6522-14250	L	5.561	0	0	0	0	0	0	0	0	0	33	5.93
163	6524-14345	L	5.554	0	0	0	0	0	0	0	0	0	34	6.12
106	6528-14310	L	5.54	0	4	1	6	0	0	0	0	11	34	6.14
141	6526-14255	L	5.547	0	0	0	1	0	0	0	0	1	34	6.13
225	6520-14345	L	5.568	0	0	0	0	0	0	0	0	0	34	6.11
137	6526-14315	H	5.547	0	0	0	0	0	0	0	0	0	34	6.13
10	6536-14330	H	5.512	0	0	0	0	0	0	0	0	0	35	6.35
34	6534-14230	H	5.519	0	0	0	0	0	0	0	0	0	35	6.34
136	6526-14320	H	5.547	0	0	0	0	1	0	0	0	2	36	6.49
71	6530-14335	L	5.533	0	0	0	0	0	0	0	0	0	36	6.51
41	6534-14145	H	5.519	0	0	1	0	0	0	0	0	1	37	6.70
21	6534-14340	H	5.519	0	0	0	0	0	0	0	0	0	37	6.70
99	6528-14345	L	5.54	0	0	0	0	0	0	0	0	0	37	6.68
149	6526-14215	L	5.547	0	0	0	0	0	0	0	0	0	37	6.67
297	6516-14300	L	5.582	1	0	1	0	1	0	0	0	4	37	6.63
174	6524-14250	L	5.554	0	0	0	0	0	0	0	0	0	38	6.84
135	6526-14325	H	5.547	0	0	0	3	0	0	0	0	3	39	7.03
144	6526-14240	L	5.547	0	0	0	0	0	0	0	0	0	39	7.03
290	6516-14335	L	5.582	0	1	0	6	0	0	0	0	7	40	7.17
64	6532-14150	H	5.526	1	2	0	5	0	0	0	0	8	40	7.24
59	6532-14225	H	5.526	0	0	0	0	0	0	0	0	0	40	7.24
33	6534-14235	H	5.519	0	1	1	0	0	0	0	0	2	41	7.43
35	6534-14225	H	5.519	0	0	0	0	1	0	0	0	2	41	7.43
58	6532-14230	H	5.526	1	0	0	0	2	0	0	0	5	41	7.42
77	6530-14305	L	5.533	1	1	0	3	0	0	0	0	5	41	7.41
55	6532-14245	H	5.526	1	0	0	0	0	0	0	0	1	43	7.78
73	6530-14325	H	5.533	3	1	1	4	0	0	0	0	9	43	7.77
36	6534-14220	L	5.519	0	2	1	0	2	0	0	0	7	44	7.97
16	6536-14230	H	5.512	1	1	2	3	0	1	0	0	10	44	7.98
239	6520-14235	L	5.568	0	0	0	0	0	0	0	0	0	48	8.62
80	6530-14250	H	5.533	1	0	0	0	1	0	0	0	3	32	5.78
84	6530-14230	L	5.533	1	0	0	1	0	0	0	0	2	38	6.87
91	6530-14155	H	5.533	0	1	1	0	1	0	0	0	4	35	6.33
92	6530-14150	H	5.533	1	1	1	2	0	0	0	0	5	35	6.33
94	6530-14140	L	5.533	0	0	0	0	0	0	0	0	0	47	8.49
116	6528-14220	L	5.54	0	0	0	0	0	0	0	0	0	37	6.68
118	6528-14210	L	5.54	0	0	0	0	0	0	0	0	0	34	6.14

Table 1 continued.

Unit	SE Corner	Stratum	Area Mi²	Bulls			Cows			Lone		Total Moose	Search Time	Effort Min/Mi²
				Yrl	Med	Lrg	0calf	1calf	2calf	Calf	Unk			
125	6528-14135	L	5.54	0	0	0	1	0	0	0	0	1	37	6.68
133	6526-14335	L	5.547	0	0	0	0	0	0	0	0	0	35	6.31
152	6526-14200	L	5.547	0	0	0	0	0	0	0	0	0	36	6.49
160	6526-14120	L	5.547	0	0	0	0	1	0	0	0	2	41	7.39
191	6524-14125	L	5.554	0	0	0	0	0	0	0	0	0	38	6.84
200	6522-14310	L	5.561	0	0	0	0	0	0	0	0	0	38	6.83
236	6520-14250	L	5.568	0	0	0	0	0	0	0	0	0	42	7.54
237	6520-14245	L	5.568	0	0	0	1	0	0	0	0	1	56	10.06
254	6520-14120	L	5.568	0	0	1	3	0	0	0	0	4	38	6.82
258	6518-14335	H	5.575	1	1	1	7	0	1	0	0	13	41	7.35
259	6518-14330	H	5.575	0	4	1	10	3	0	0	0	21	39	7.00
260	6518-14325	H	5.575	0	2	2	1	1	0	0	0	7	39	7.00
283	6518-14130	H	5.575	0	0	0	0	2	0	0	0	4	40	7.17
284	6518-14125	H	5.575	0	5	3	3	0	1	0	0	14	40	7.17
300	6516-14245	L	5.582	0	0	0	0	0	0	0	0	0	59	10.57
311	6516-14150	L	5.582	0	1	0	0	2	0	0	0	5	40	7.17
315	6516-14130	H	5.582	0	0	0	1	0	0	0	0	1	32	5.73
316	6516-14125	H	5.582	0	2	2	3	0	0	0	0	7	32	5.73
325	6514-14315	L	5.589	0	0	0	0	0	0	0	0	0	42	7.51
330	6514-14250	L	5.589	0	0	0	0	0	0	0	0	0	50	8.95
340	6514-14200	L	5.589	0	0	0	0	0	0	0	0	0	27	4.83
364	6512-14225	H	5.596	0	0	0	0	0	0	0	0	0	39	6.97
365	6512-14220	H	5.596	0	0	0	0	0	0	0	0	0	40	7.15
367	6512-14210	H	5.596	0	2	0	7	0	0	0	0	9	39	6.97
368	6512-14205	H	5.596	0	2	0	2	2	0	0	0	8	43	7.68
369	6512-14200	H	5.596	0	1	1	1	0	0	0	0	3	28	5.00
373	6512-14140	L	5.596	0	0	0	0	0	0	0	0	0	38	6.79
383	6510-14315	L	5.603	0	0	0	1	0	0	0	0	1	51	9.10
390	6510-14240	H	5.603	0	0	0	1	0	0	0	0	1	40	7.14
392	6510-14230	H	5.603	0	0	0	0	0	0	0	0	0	48	8.57
396	6510-14210	H	5.603	0	0	0	0	0	0	0	0	0	24	4.28
397	6510-14205	H	5.603	0	0	0	6	0	0	0	0	6	47	8.39
401	6510-14145	L	5.603	0	0	0	0	0	0	0	0	0	28	5.00
403	6510-14135	L	5.603	0	0	0	0	0	1	0	0	3	35	6.25
413	6508-14310	L	5.61	0	0	0	1	1	0	0	0	3	43	7.66
415	6508-14300	L	5.61	0	0	0	0	0	0	0	0	0	43	7.66
417	6508-14250	L	5.61	0	0	0	4	0	0	0	0	4	59	10.52
419	6508-14240	H	5.61	0	0	0	0	0	0	0	0	0	40	7.13
429	6508-14150	H	5.61	0	0	0	1	0	0	0	0	1	38	6.77
440	6506-14315	L	5.617	0	0	0	0	0	0	0	0	0	41	7.30
450	6506-14225	H	5.617	1	0	2	2	0	0	0	0	5	50	8.90
477	6504-14225	L	5.624	0	0	0	1	0	0	0	0	1	45	8.00
483	6504-14155	H	5.624	0	0	0	0	0	0	0	0	0	20	3.56
485	6504-14145	H	5.624	0	0	2	0	0	0	0	0	2	28	4.98
488	6504-14130	L	5.624	0	0	0	0	0	0	0	0	0	30	5.33
498	6502-14255	H	5.631	0	0	0	0	0	0	0	0	0	41	7.28
501	6502-14240	L	5.631	0	0	0	1	0	0	0	0	1	53	9.41
506	6502-14215	L	5.631	0	0	0	0	0	0	0	0	0	26	4.62
508	6502-14205	H	5.631	0	0	0	0	0	0	0	0	0	31	5.51
514	6502-14135	H	5.631	0	0	0	1	2	0	0	0	5	33	5.86
515	6502-14130	H	5.631	0	0	0	0	0	0	0	0	0	26	4.62
517	6502-14120	L	5.631	0	0	0	0	0	0	0	0	0	32	5.68
522	6500-14255	H	5.638	0	0	3	3	1	0	0	0	8	48	8.51

Table 1 continued.

Unit	SE Corner	Stratum	Area Mi²	Bulls Yrl	Bulls Med	Bulls Lrg	Cows 0calf	Cows 1calf	Cows 2calf f	Lone Calf	Unk	Total Moose	Search Time	Effort Min/Mi²
523	6500-14250	H	5.638	0	0	1	0	1	0	0	0	3	42	7.45
535	6500-14150	H	5.638	0	3	0	1	2	0	0	0	8	30	5.32
536	6500-14145	H	5.638	1	3	0	0	3	0	0	0	10	31	5.50
537	6500-14140	H	5.638	0	0	0	5	0	0	0	0	5	37	6.56
538	6500-14135	H	5.638	1	0	0	8	1	0	0	0	11	51	9.05
544	6500-14105	L	5.638	0	0	0	0	0	0	0	0	0	30	5.32
554	6458-14150	L	5.645	0	0	0	0	0	0	0	0	0	18	3.19
555	6458-14145	H	5.645	3	2	0	2	1	0	0	0	9	28	4.96
557	6458-14135	H	5.645	0	4	0	6	0	0	0	0	10	56	9.92
560	6458-14120	L	5.645	0	0	0	0	0	0	0	0	0	33	5.85
	Total		618.77	21	52	29	126	34	4	0	0	308	4158	745.88253
	Average												37.46	6.72

Table 2. November 2009, moose survey population estimate, Yukon-Charley Rivers National Preserve, Alaska. Results from the GeoSpatial Estimator. Also see the GeoSpatial Estimator output in Appendix A.

STRATUM	LOW	HIGH	TOTAL
Total no. of survey units	394	161	555
Total area (mi²)	2197	899	3096
No. of units surveyed	59	52	111
Area surveyed (mi²)	540	301	841
No. of moose seen	80	228	308
Density with 1.2 SCF			0.429
Point Estimate with 1.2 SCF			1331
Estimate Standard Error			127.34

Estimates with no SCF applied: Point Estimate = 1109.317
80% Confidence Interval = (946, 1273) = +/- 163 = +/- 14.71%
90% Confidence Interval = (900, 1319) = +/- 209 = +/- 18.88%
95% Confidence Interval = (860, 1359) = +/- 249 = +/- 22.49%
(no SCF)

Sex and Age Composition

The sex and age composition of the 308 observed moose were as follows: 164 cows, 102 bulls, and 42 calves. Composition of the observed bulls included an unusually high 21 yearling bulls (spiked or forked antlers), 52 medium bulls, and 29 large bulls. No single-antlered bulls were seen, therefore antler shed did not appear to be a problem. Bulls begin to lose their antlers in late November. If surveys are conducted much later than early December sex ratios can become increasingly inaccurate and are even more difficult in a spring (March) survey because cows can only be identified from bulls consistently by seeing the white vulva patch. Accomplishing this from aircraft is often very difficult to do.

11

The estimated sex and age ratios of the population were 26 calves:100 cows, 13 spike/fork (yearling bulls):100 cows, and 59 bulls:100 cows, twinning rate was 2.65 sets of twins:100 cows. During this November 2009 survey 4 sets of twins were seen (Table 3).

Table 3. Number of sets of twins seen during past moose surveys.

Survey Year	Sets of twins seen
1994	1
1997	3
1999	6
2003	1
2006	5
2009	4
Average	3.3

The total number of yearlings is estimated by doubling the number of yearling bulls, assuming a 50:50 sex ratio. This would make the ratio 27 yearlings:100 cows. However, the yearling component of the population is likely under-estimated because we only classified those bulls with spike or forked antlers as yearlings. Studies conducted by ADF&G indicate that yearling bulls can grow larger palmated antlers up to 30 inches (76 cm), and spike/fork bulls may represent only 40%-60% of the yearling cohort in a given year assuming adequate nutrition (Gasaway et al. 1983, Gasaway et al. 1992). Therefore, if we assume that spike/fork bulls represent 60% of the yearling cohort in YUCH, an additional 40% would increase the total number of yearling bulls to 120 and the total number of yearlings to 240. The ratios would increase to 16.7 yearling bulls:100 cows, or 40 total yearlings:100 cows.

Comparisons and Trends

Several moose surveys have been conducted in the past in YUCH (Table 4). However, study objectives and budget constraints resulted in a different sampling technique in 1987 and a different survey area (although overlapping) and much shorter search intensity for the 1994 survey. Comparisons of the earlier surveys (1987 and 1994) with the last five (1997, 1999, 2003, 2006, 2009) are difficult and perhaps inappropriate, because comparing these data may result in misleading or erroneous conclusions. The aerial moose surveys conducted in November 1997, 1999, 2003, 2006, and 2009 covered the same area, using directly comparable methods. The 1994, 1997 and 1999 surveys used techniques based on Gasaway et al.(1986). The 2003, 2006, and 2009 surveys also used the techniques based on Gasaway et al. (1986) but as modified by Ver Hoef (2001) into the Geo Spatial technique (DeLong 2006, Kellie and DeLong 2006).

Table 4. November moose survey data from past years for Yukon-Charley Rivers National Preserve, Alaska. Population estimates for 1987 and 1994 data are not directly comparable to 1997, 1999, 2003, 2006, and 2009. Composition ratios are comparable.

Year	Bull:Cow ratio	Calf:Cow ratio	Yrlbull:Cow ratio[1]	Density moose/mi^2	Population estimate (90% CI)
1987[2]	121	10	14	0.62	1116 (no CI)
1994[2]	84	21	7	0.31	735 (+/-166)
1997	60	28	8	0.27	737 (+/-148)
1999	51	36	5	0.36	979 (+/- 188)
2003[3]	61	25	6	0.265	835 (+/- 199)
2006[3]	73	33	7	0.234	726 (+/- 139)
2009[3]	59	26	12	0.429	1331 (+/- 209)

[1] spike fork bulls only, not corrected

[2] not directly comparable with later surveys

[3] SCF of 1.2 applied to Geo Spatial Estimates. Gassaway estimates have their respective SCFs

The primary differences between the 1994 survey and the surveys that followed, were search intensity and boundaries of the survey area. The 1994 survey was conducted at a lower search intensity (about 1 minute/mi^2 (Dale et al. 1994). Moose density in the 1200 mi^2 overlap area was estimated at 0.34 moose/mi^2 during 1994, 0.23 moose/mi^2 during 1997, and 0.23 moose/mi^2 for the 1999 survey (Burch 1999). For the first time in 2009 a significant increase can be measured in the moose population between 2006 and 2009 as illustrated by non-overlapping confidence intervals between those 2 surveys (Table 4, Figure 5). Variation in moose densities between years could be the result of many things including immigration and emigration, changes in survival due to snow depth, changes in habitat and forage quantity and quality often due to wildland fire and succession of browse species, and predation by both wolves and bears. These data will become more valuable when combined with future years of comparable data collected within the framework of the long-term monitoring program of the Central Alaska Network. This will allow identification of trends in YUCH moose densities, and help begin to determine the primary limiting factors of YUCH's moose population.

Moose densities in YUCH (at 0.429 moose/mi^2) are among the lowest reported in the region, and age and sex ratios of the moose population in YUCH are typical of other low-density populations in interior Alaska (Gasaway et al. 1992). In another portion of GMU 20E (Tok West) the overall moose density in November 2006 was 0.98 moose/mi^2 with 37 calves and 39 bulls per 100 cows (Jeff Gross pers. comm. 2007). In Denali National Park (a predominately unhunted population of moose) an 2004 survey found an overall density of 0.29 moose per square mile and 39 calves and 88 bulls per 100 cows (Owen and Meier 2005). A 2008 survey in Denali found 0.33 moose per square mile with 24 calves and 54 bulls per 100 cows (Owen and Meier 2009). In GMUs 25A, 25B, 25D (down the Yukon River from YUCH) moose densities were 0.6 moose/mi^2 with 30 calves and 50 bulls per 100 cows (Stephenson 1996). A survey conducted in Western Yukon Flats National Wildlife Refuge in November of 2004 reported a density of 0.23 moose/mi^2 and 35 calves and 72 bulls per 100 cows, and in November 2001 reported 0.29 moose/mi^2 with 52 bulls and 27 calves per 100 cows (Bertram 2005). This is in contrast with GMU 20A south of Fairbanks where moose densities have been much higher at 3.1 moose/mi^2 and 34 calves and 39 bulls per 100 cows for November 2006 (Don Young, pers. comm. 2007).

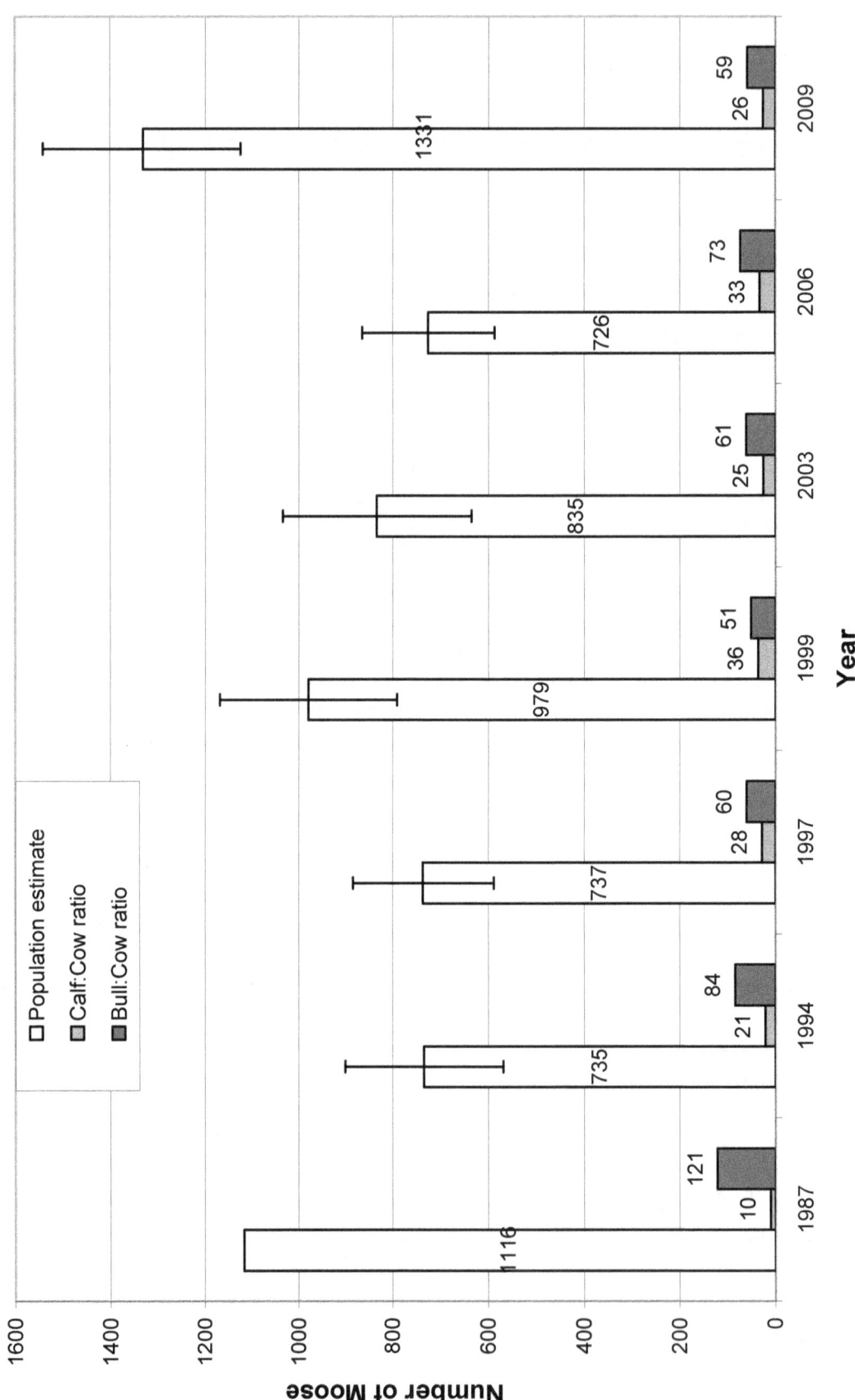

Figure 5. Trends in moose population size, calf:cow ratios and bull:cow ratios 1987 – 2009. Yukon-Charley Rivers National Preserve, Alaska. A sightability correction factor applied to all estimates including the 2003 - 2009 Geo Spatial estimates.

Harvest

Moose harvest and hunter success from 1983 to 2007 was summarized from ADF&G harvest data (Table 4 and Figure 6). Harvest data from 2008 and 2009 were not available at the time of this writing. The area covered includes all Uniform Coding Units (UCUs) within the 3 Game Management Units (GMU) and subunits that are completely or partially within YUCH (Figure 7). Moose harvest in YUCH has averaged 26 bulls/yr over the past 24 years (range 12-41, SE=2.08) and there has been a significant increase in moose harvest overall (r^2= 0.434, F=13.83, p=0.002, α =0.05). The average moose harvest for the first 10 years (Av=19.8, SE=2.39) is significantly lower than the average of the last 10 years (Av=28.4, SE=1.94; t=-4.43, p<0.0017, α =0.05). These tests indicate a significant increase in the number of moose harvested since 1983. During 1983-2006, an average of 92 hunters (range 41-168, SE=6.59) hunted moose in the preserve each year, spending an average of 7 - 8 days per hunt. Comparing the average number of hunters from the first 10 years (65) to the last 10 years (110) indicates a significant increase in the number of people hunting in the preserve (t=-6.99, p<0.001, α =0.05). Furthermore, there is also a significant trend in the increase in the number of hunters over the 24 year period (r^2=0.77, F=58.58, p<0.001, α=0.05). Reported hunter success has averaged 32% (range 12-46%) during this 24 year period. Average hunter success during the first 10 years (31.8) is not significantly different from the last 10 years (27.1; t=0.219, p=0.832, α =0.05) showing the success of hunters has remained about the same, even though the average number of hunters has increased. Moose hunting in the preserve occurs primarily along the main rivers such as the Yukon, Kandik, Nation, and Charley Rivers. Hunters also use airstrips and remote landing areas within YUCH, but few moose are harvested considerable distances from the main rivers (Fig. 7).

Table 4. Reported moose harvest, number of hunters, hunter effort and success in Yukon-Charley Rivers National Preserve, Alaska, 1983 to 2007. Harvest data from 2008 and 2009 were not yet available from ADF&G.

Year	Moose Harvested	Number of Hunters	Percent Success	Hunter Effort Days/Moose	Hunter Days
1983	21	59	36	28	597
1984	19	46	41	17	326
1985	19	41	46	21	399
1986	13	48	27	20	260
1987	14	57	25	30	413
1988	17	66	26	27	464
1989	17	61	28	28	476
1990	35	81	43	15	538
1991	31	90	34	24	747
1992	12	100	12	62	739
1993	36	93	39	20	719
1994	32	126	25	29	926
1995	33	99	33	24	797
1996	24	94	26	33	793
1997	24	100	24	35	851
1998	37	80	46	22	828
1999	41	116	35	24	987
2000	38	102	37	23	873
2001	25	145	17	45	1117
2002	34	129	26	28	952
2003	20	168	12	N/A	N/A
2004	26	104	25	N/A	N/A
2005	23	77	30	21	479
2006	26	97	27	23	603
2007	23	115	20	41	944
Total	640	2294	741	641	15828
Mean	25.6	91.8	29.6	27.9	688.2
first 10yr mean	19.8	64.9	31.8	27.2	495.9
last 10yr mean	28.4	110.6	27.1	29.6	842.7
last 5yr mean	25.3	119.3	22.5	31.5	819.0

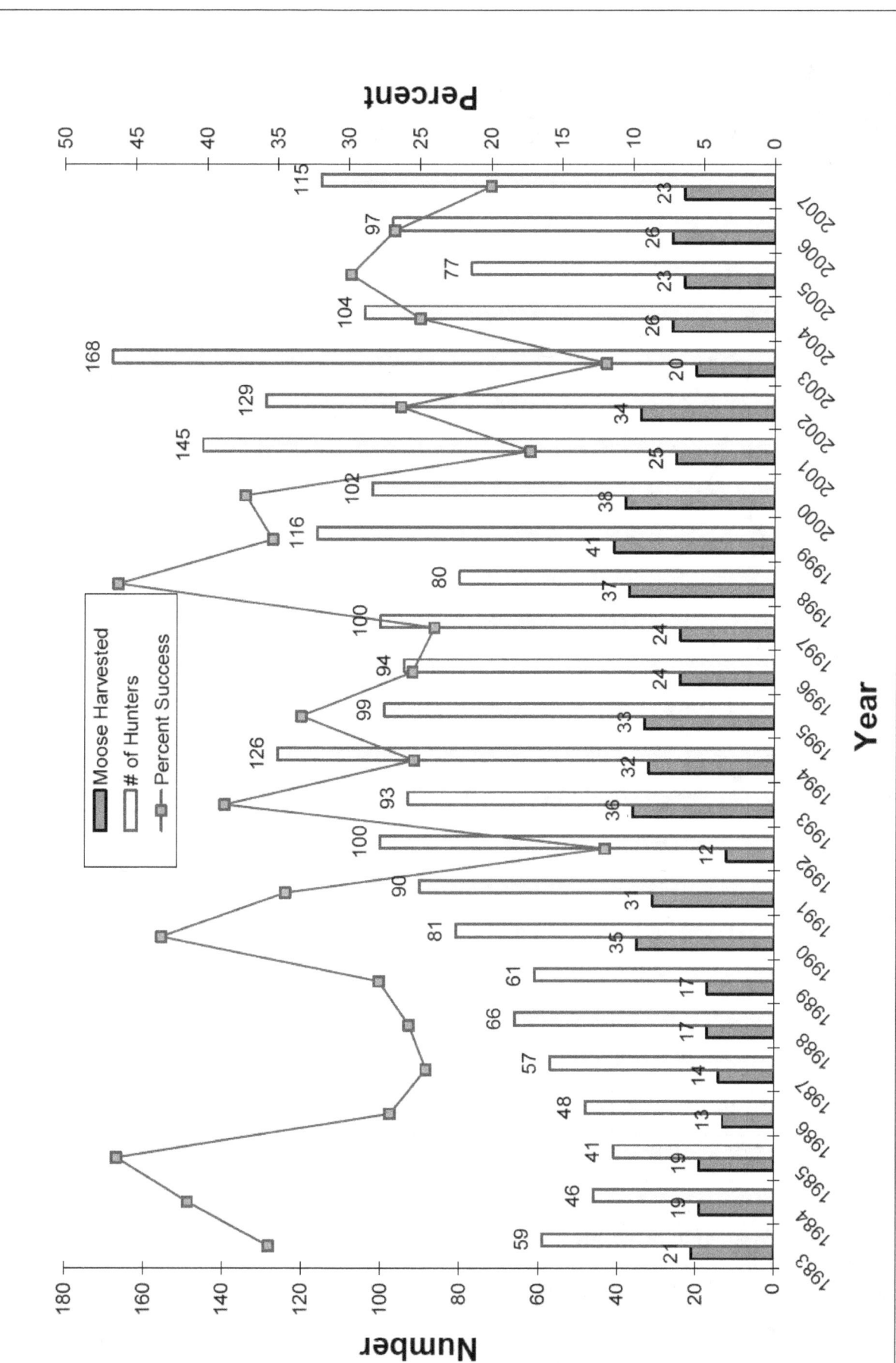

Figure 6. Reported moose harvest, number of hunters, and hunter success in Yukon-Charley Rivers National Preserve, Alaska, 1983- 2007 (data gathered from ADF&G harvest reports, 2008 and 2009 data were not available).

17

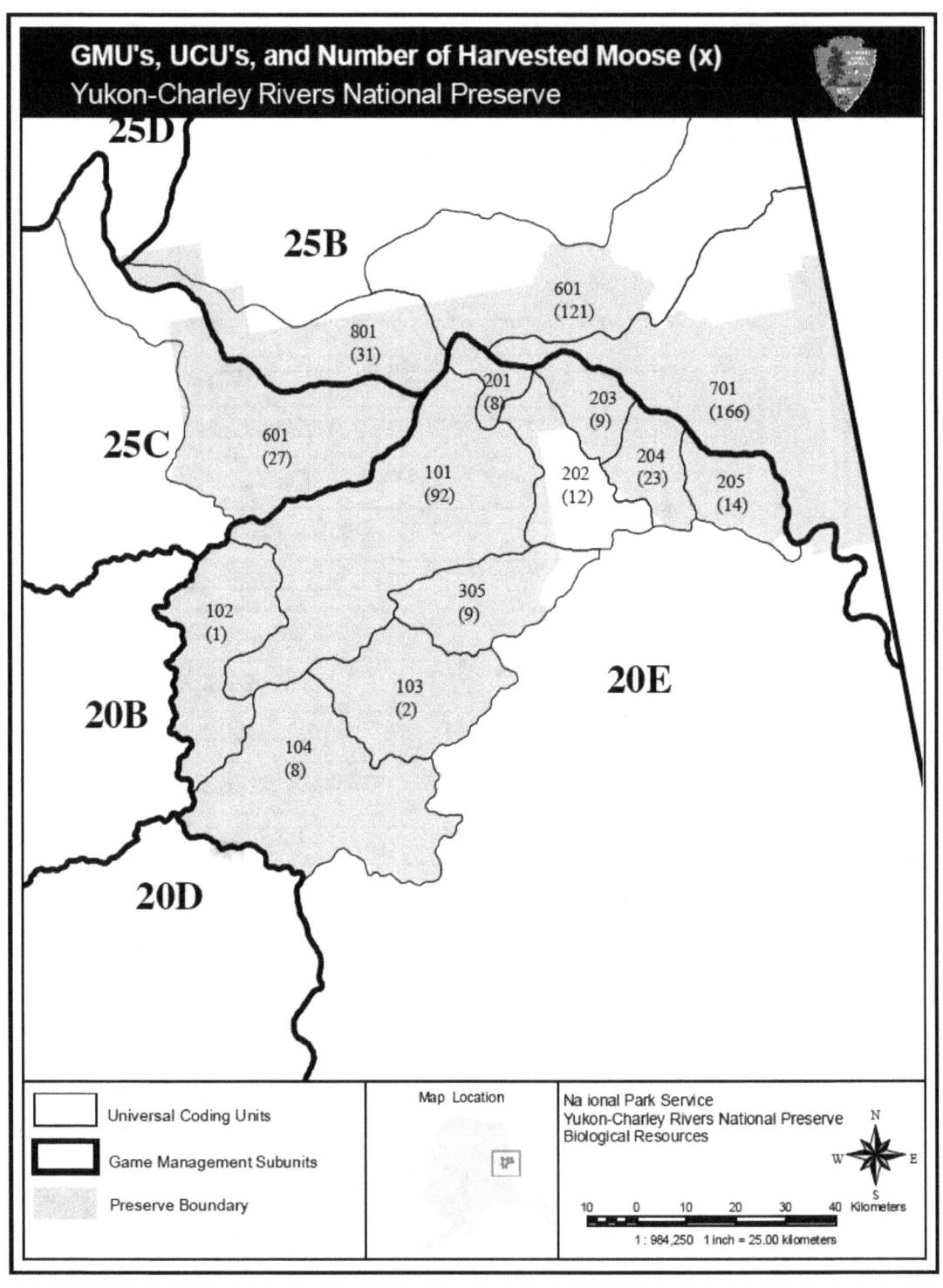

Figure 7. Game management subunits and uniform coding units (UCUs) comprising Yukon-Charley Rivers National Preserve, Alaska. Numbers in parentheses are number of moose reported harvested from 1983-2007 for each UCU.

Natural Mortality

We know very little about the natural mortality of moose in YUCH. Nearby studies over past years indicate that predation by both black and brown bears on newborn calves can be significant in the spring, and wolf predation on calves and adults is significant. From 1981-1988, ADF&G intensively studied the moose population in the Fortymile drainage south of YUCH where, in a study of 33 radiocollared newborn calves, 82% died within 11 months (52% by grizzly bears, 15% by wolves, 3% by black bears, and 12% drowned) (Gasaway et al. 1992). In the same study they found survival rates of adult moose to range from 78% to 93%. In 1998 and 1999 in Yukon Flats National Wildlife Refuge, data from a moose calf mortality study found 32 of 80 (40%) collared calves were killed by bears (17 by black bears, 15 by brown bears) and only a single calf was known to have been killed by a wolf, although there were 26 mortalities of unknown cause (Bertram and Vivion 2002). A moose study in Denali National Park and Preserve calculated survival rates for adult cows at 86%, 88%, and 94% for the years 2000, 2001, 2002 respectively, but causes of mortality were not identified (Layne Adams, USGS/BRD personal communication, 2004).

Wolf predation is a common cause of death of adult moose as well as calves in YUCH (Burch 2002, 2008, 2009). During routine radiotracking flights from an on-going wolf study in YUCH, there has been no significant trend in locations of wolves on moose kills from 1993 – 2009 ($r^2 = 0.027$, F=0.335 p=0.56, α=0.05) (Table 5) (Burch 2002, 2008, 2009).

Table 5. Number of moose kills observed with radiocollared wolf packs.

Biological Year	Number of VHF Locations	Moose Kills	% Moose Kills
92-93	63	1	1.6
93-94	301	18	6.0
94-95	289	19	6.6
95-96	158	6	3.8
96-97	158	17	10.8
97-98	442	15	3.4
98-99	387	8	2.1
99-00	369	5	1.4
00-01	267	10	3.7
01-02	339	20	5.9
02-03	152	3	2.0
03-04*	56	2	3.6
04-05*	72	3	4.2
05-06	130	9	6.9
06-07	197	12	6.1
07-08	181	11	6.1
08-09	183	13	7.1

* very few radiotelemetry flights due to budget constraints.

Distribution of Moose

From the survey locations of moose groups in November it appears that moose congregate in the hills on either side of the Yukon in the late fall. This is illustrated by the distribution of moose groups from the 1997, 1999, 2003, 2006, and 2009 surveys (locations covering only the moose survey area), and the distribution of wolf-killed moose from 1993-2009 throughout YUCH (Figure 8). Assuming that most moose are shot near the Yukon River or its major tributaries in September, this could indicate moose migrating into the hills in the late fall, or that one portion of the population is absorbing the majority of the harvest. It is possible some moose may move farther, and the population in the Yukon valley during the September hunt is higher than indicated by moose surveys in November. The scatter of wolf- killed moose throughout the preserve and beyond gives some idea of moose distribution outside the surveyed areas (Figure 8). When the wolf-killed moose locations are viewed alone, it shows a preponderance of moose in the hills of the Yukon Valley and fewer moose kills in the upper Charley River area. This coincides with local knowledge, human harvest locations, and the 1994 moose survey, all indicating fewer moose in the upper Charley.

With the wildfires that have occurred in YUCH in the past decade it is easy to speculate that those fires had some influence on the increase in moose in the area, and perhaps they have. A quick look at the distribution of known moose locations with past fire history appears to show some correlation between past fires and moose distribution (Figure 9). However it is not a simple cause and effect as there are definite places that have concentrations of moose that have no record of a wildland fire occurring at least back to the 1940's. Furthermore, there are areas that have been burned at various times where few or no moose have been seen. The subject is not a simple one and beyond the scope of this report. A more thorough analysis is planned later in 2010 (Jennifer Allen, NPS Fire Ecologist, personal communication).

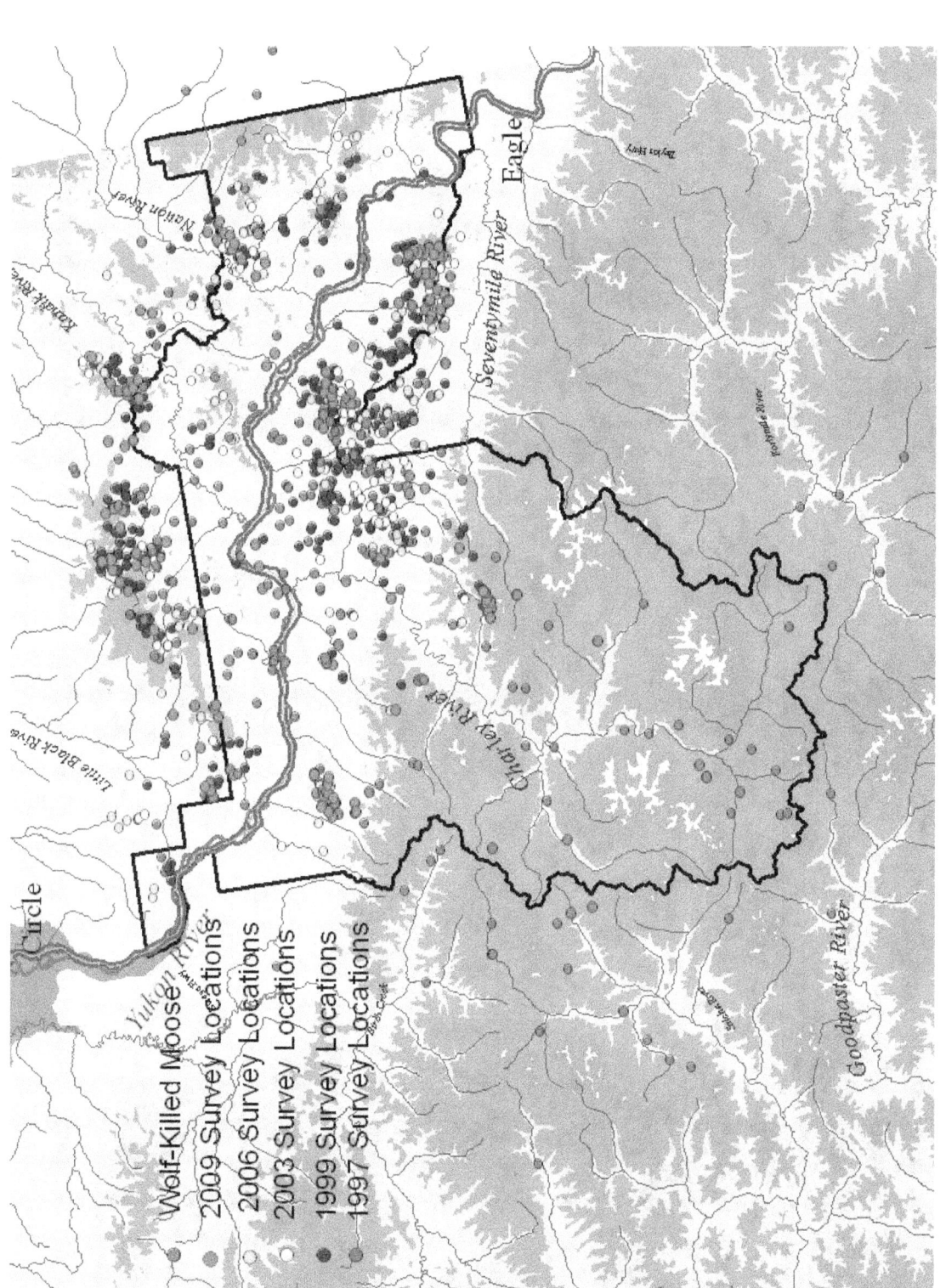

Figure 8. Distribution of moose group locations from 1997, 1999, 2003, 2006, and 2009 surveys and the distribution of wolf-killed moose (red dots) from 1993-2009, in Yukon-Charley Rivers National Preserve, Alaska.

21

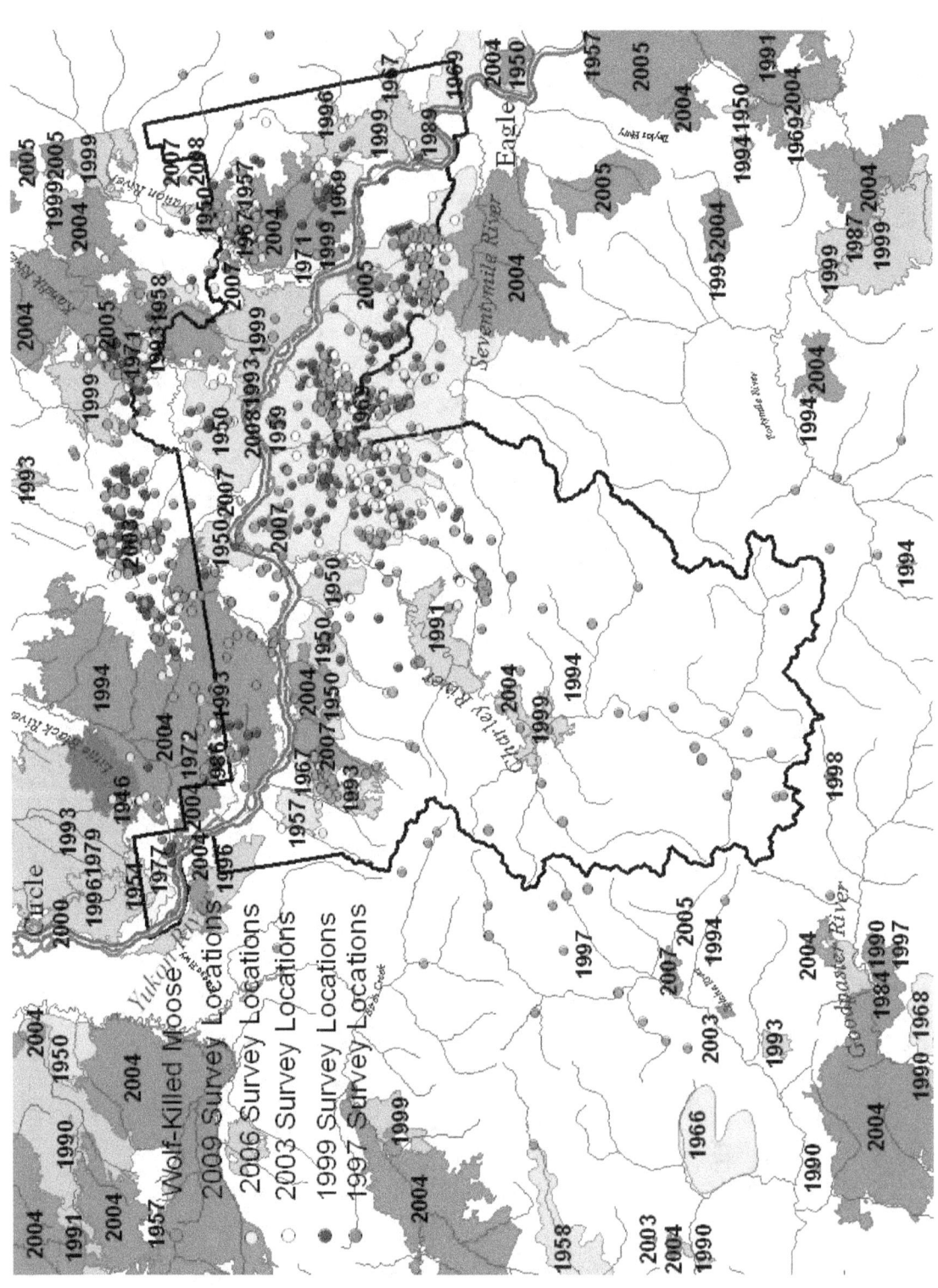

Figure 9. Distribution of moose from past surveys and wolf kills and Fire history of the area (boundaries of more recent fires obscure the boundaries of older fires). Yukon-Charley Rivers National Preserve, Alaska.

Conclusions and Management Recommendations

The point estimate of the overall density of 0.429 moose/mi^2 is nearly twice that of previous surveys which were among the lowest reported in interior Alaska (Gasaway et al. 1992). However, when the confidence intervals of all surveys are taken into consideration, one cannot say the population doubled with any statistical rigor, but it did increase. The population estimates and sex and age composition of the YUCH moose population appear consistent with a low density, stable population. There was an unusually high number of yearling bulls seen on this survey (21 observed, 86 in the population estimate) when compared to previous surveys, indicating a bumper crop of calves in spring 2008 and /or excellent survival of those calves.

While the number of hunters has increased since the early 1980s, hunter success rates have remained comparable to the 20 year average. A proposal to lengthen the federal subsistence hunting season on bulls and to remove antler size restrictions for harvestable bulls was adopted in 1998, changing the season dates within YUCH. Since 1998, federal subsistence regulations now include August 29-31 making a subsistence season that extends from August 20 to September 30 for any bull (a change from one bull with spike-fork antlers from August 20-August 28, and no season from August 29-August 31). A proposed March hunting season was not adopted but could be proposed again in the future. The YUCH moose population could be at the maximum sustainable harvest levels right now. Extending hunting seasons to include a March season, (or the harvest of any cows) could increase harvest enough to adversely affect YUCH's moose population despite the recent, modest increase in moose numbers.

Another factor complicating moose management in YUCH is the lack of knowledge of moose movements in and adjacent to YUCH. Studies of other moose populations in interior Alaska have documented significant moose movements (Hobgood and Durtsche 1990, Gasaway 1992, Dale and Boertje unpublished data). Some of these movements are migratory in nature and occur seasonally (spring and fall). Anecdotal information suggests that snow and other factors may influence the timing and magnitude of movements. These movements could affect the results of moose surveys, and the November survey results may not be representative of the moose population during the August/September moose hunt. Information on the timing and extent of any moose movements within and adjacent to YUCH is critical in order for managers to develop and implement an appropriate monitoring protocol that will contribute to science-based management decisions.

Available moose population information for YUCH is adequate for past management decisions, but surveys need to continue for future management decision making. A long-term monitoring program with consistent sampling techniques has been implemented to track the status of the YUCH moose population, through the vital signs monitoring program of the Central Alaska Network. A Geo Spatial population survey modeled after Gasaway et al. (1986) and modified by Ver Hoef (2001) (Kellie and DeLong 2006) should be conducted every 3 years, and would cost about $25,000 – $30,000 per survey. The next survey should occur in fall 2012. This monitoring level would provide managers with statistically reliable population estimates and a consistent means to estimate sex and age composition. In addition, a study of moose movements in YUCH would provide valuable information to assist in determining an appropriate population monitoring protocol and allow managers to make informed decisions regarding moose management to maintain healthy populations for future generations.

Literature Cited

Alaska Department of Fish and Game. 1995. Fortymile Caribou Herd management plan. 21pp.

Alaska Department of Fish and Game. 2006. Fortymile Caribou Herd Harvest plan. 13pp.

Bertram, M. 2005. Moose population survey Western Yukon Flats. Survey Report. 18pp.

Bertram, M. and M. Vivion. 2002. Moose mortality in Eastern Interior Alaska. Journal of Wildlife Management 66(3):747-756.

Boertje, R. D. 1985. Letter to Steve Ulvi, National Park Service. April 9, 1985. Alaska Department of Fish and Game. 2pp.

Burch, J. W. and N. J. Demma. 1997. 1997 Aerial moose survey along the Yukon River corridor, Yukon-Charley Rivers National Preserve, Alaska. NPS Technical Report NPS/AR/NRTR-98/33. 23pp.

Burch, J. W. 1999. 1999 aerial moose survey along the Yukon River corridor, Yukon-Charley Rivers National Preserve, Alaska. NPS Technical Report NPS/AR/NRNT-2002/40. 25pp.

Burch, J. W. 2002. Ecology and demography of wolves in Yukon-Charley Rivers National Preserve, Alaska. NPS Technical Report NPS/AR/NRTR-2001/41. 72pp.

Burch, J. W. 2003. 2003 aerial moose survey along the Yukon River corridor, Yukon-Charley Rivers National Preserve, Alaska. NPS Technical Report NPS/AR/NRNT-2004/44. 27pp

Burch, J. W. 2006. 2006 aerial moose survey along the Yukon River corridor, Yukon-Charley Rivers National Preserve, Alaska. Natural Resource Technical Report NPS/CAKN/NRTR—2006. National Park Service, Fort Collins, Colorado. 36pp

Burch, J. W. 2008. Annual report on vital signs monitoring of wolf (*Canis lupus*) distribution and abundance in Yukon-Charley Rivers National Preserve, Central Alaska Network: 2008 report. Natural Resource Technical Report NPS/CAKN/NRTR—2008/149. National Park Service, Fort Collins, Colorado.

Burch, J. W. 2009. Annual report on vital signs monitoring of wolf (*Canis lupus*) distribution and abundance in Yukon-Charley Rivers National Preserve, Central Alaska Network: 2009 report. Natural Resource Technical Report NPS/CAKN/NRTR—2009/228. National Park Service, Fort Collins, Colorado.

Demma, N. J., B. W. Dale, and K. B. Fox. 1995. 1994 Aerial moose survey, Yukon-Charley Rivers National Preserve, Alaska. NPS Tech Report NPS/ARRNR/NRTR-95/26. 14pp.

Dale, B. W. 1996. 1996 moose management report (20A). Alaska Department of Fish and Game report, Fairbanks, Alaska. 15 pp.

Dale, B. W., L. G. Adams, and W. T. Route. 1994. A relatively inexpensive aerial moose survey
technique designed as a replacement for trend surveys or for the use in areas with high sightability. NPS Natural Resources Report AR-94. 15 pp.

DeLong R. A. 2006. GeoSpatial population estimator software user's guide. Alaska Department of Fish and Game, Fairbanks, Alaska, USA. 72pp.

Gardner, C. L. 1996. 1996 Moose management report (20E). Alaska Department of Fish and Game report, Fairbanks AK.14pp.

Gasaway, W. C., R. D. Boertje, D. V. Grangaard, D. G. Kelleyhouse, R. O. Stephenson, and D. G
Larson. 1992. The role of predation in limiting moose at low densities in Alaska and Yukon and implications for conservation. Wildlife Monograph 120. 59pp.

Gasaway, W. C., S. D. Dubois, D. J. Reed, and S. J. Harbo. 1986. Estimating moose population parameters from aerial surveys. Biological Papers, University of Alaska. No. 22. 108pp.

Gasaway, W. C. R. O. Stephenson, J. L. Davis, P. E. K. Shepherd, and O. E. Burris. 1983. Interrelationships of wolves, prey, and man in interior Alaska. Wildlife Monograph 84. 50 pp.

Hobgood, W., and B. M. Durtsche. 1990. Ecology of moose in the White Mountains National Recreation Area, Alaska, 1985-88. BLM-Alaska Open File Report. No. 27. 17pp.

Kellie K. A. and R. A. DeLong. 2006. Geospatial survey operations manual. Alaska Department of Fish and Game. Fairbanks, Alaska, USA. 55pp.

Knuckles, P. 1991. Moose winter habitat survey, Nation River, Yukon-Charley Rivers National Preserve. NPS research and resource management report series 91-02. 4pp.

Meier, T. J., J. A. Keay, J. C. VanHorn, J. W. Burch. 1991. 1991 Aerial moose survey, Denali National Park and Preserve. National Park Service Natural Resources Survey and Inventory Report AR-91/06. 19pp.

National Park Service. 1985. Yukon-Charley Rivers National Preserve general management plan. Preserve files, Fairbanks, Alaska. 147pp.

National Park Service. 1999. Fire management plan for Yukon-Charley Rivers National Preserve, Alaska. Preserve files, Fairbanks, Alaska. 50pp.

National Park Service, 2003. Subsistence management plan, Denali National Park and Preserve.

Nowlin, R. 1988. Summary of Yukon-Charley Rivers Preserve moose survey results conducted by ADF&G and NPS during November 1987. Preserve files, Fairbanks, Alaska. 15pp.

Owen, P. A. and T. J. Meier. 2005. 2004 Aerial Moose Survey, Denali National Park and Preserve. National Park Service, Denali Park, Alaska. 7pp.

Owen, P.A. and T.J. Meier. 2009. 2008 Aerial Moose Survey, Denali National Park and Preserve. National Park Service, Denali Park, Alaska. 12 pp.

Reed, D. J. 1989. Moosepop program documentation and instructions. Alaska Department of Fish and Game. 15pp.

Stephenson, R. O. 1996. 1996 Moose management report (25A,25B, and 25D). Alaska Department of Fish and Game report, Fairbanks, Alaska. 25pp.

Swanson, D. K. 1999. Ecological units of Yukon-Charley Rivers National Preserve, Alaska. National Park Service report YUCH-99-001, Fairbanks, Alaska. 31pp.

Ver Hoef, J. M. 2001. Predicting finite populations from spatially correlated data. 2000. Proceedings of the section on Statistics and the Environment of the American Statistical Association, pp. 93-98.

Ver Hoef, J. M. 2002. Sampling and geostatistics for spatial data. Ecoscience 9: 152-161.

Appendix A. Output from the Geospatial population estimator software (Ver Hoef 2001, DeLong 2006, Kellie and DeLong 2006). No sightability correction factor (SCF) applied.

RESULTS				
Estimate		**Confidence Intervals**		
Population Estimate:	1109.317	Confidence	Interval (moose)	Interval (proportion of the mean)
Standard Error:	127.3377	80%	946.127 1272.507	0.1471084
		90%	899.8649 1318.7686	0.1888116
		95%	859.7394 1358.8940	0.2249829

SAMPLE DETAILS			
Total Samples	Stratum N 1 High 161 2 Low 394 3 TOTAL 555	Total Area	Stratum Area 1 High 898.769 2 Low 2197.037 3 TOTAL 3095.806
Sample Sizes	Stratum n 1 High 52 2 Low 59 3 TOTAL 111	Area Sampled	Stratum Area 1 High 290.149 2 Low 328.563 3 TOTAL 618.712
Moose Counted	Stratum Counted 1 High 228 2 Low 80 3 TOTAL 308		

ESTIMATE DETAILS		
Stratum	High	Low
Empirical Semi-Variogram	distance gamma np 1 4.425088 0.4891831 108 2 9.639980 0.4221646 136 3 15.670181 0.7424979 106 4 21.849362 0.5819074 138 5 28.722070 0.5362052 176 6 34.241439 0.5417309 214 7 40.865444 0.6755294 278 8 46.905169 0.6263317 264	distance gamma np 1 4.814794 0.1107483 46 2 9.948848 0.1839852 174 3 15.396777 0.2419472 164 4 21.749884 0.2233081 272 5 28.263479 0.2168474 318 6 34.507710 0.1751042 312 7 40.683628 0.1594449 336 8 46.868649 0.1236007 260
Parameter Estimates	nugget parsil range 1 3.164508e-06 0.6810778 4.013476	nugget parsil range 1 5.891878e-08 0.1602728 4.345015

Sampling and Stratification

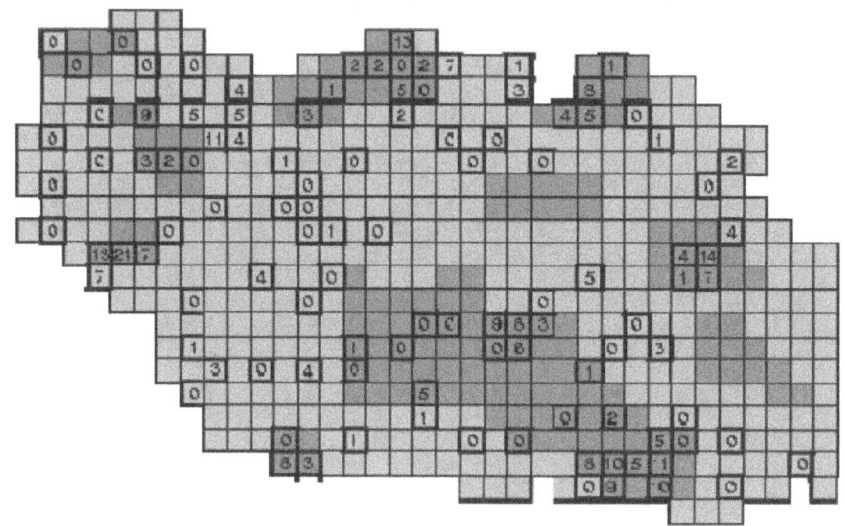

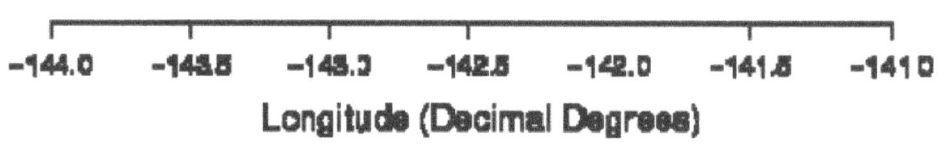

Longitude (Decimal Degrees)

NPS 191/102388, May 2010